From Broken to Blessed

An Attempt at Suicide that Ended with Blessings beyond My Dreams

JEROME PETTY

ISBN 979-8-88832-184-3 (paperback)
ISBN 979-8-88832-185-0 (digital)

Christian Faith Publishing
832 Park Avenue
Meadville, PA 16335
www.christianfaithpublishing.com

Printed in the United States of America

I would like to dedicate this book, which is my story, my struggles, and my triumphs, to God Almighty. Thank you for ordering my steps and opening my mind to the truth. Thank you for choosing me for this journey, the good and the bad. Please continue to have your way with your servant. I pray that this book brings honor and glory to your name, in Jesus's name. You are the true author behind this story, which has a triumphant ending as long as I follow the script.

I would also like to dedicate this book to my mother. The hard work you did to raise us did not go unnoticed, and for the remainder of my life, I will be working hard to see to it that you will not need for anything!

INTRODUCTION

I had fainted, unless I had believed to see the goodness of the Lord
in the land of the living. Wait on the Lord: Be of good courage,
and he shall strengthen thine heart: Wait I say on the Lord.

—Psalm 27:13–14

There was no relief from the constant painful thoughts that replayed
itself over and over again in my mind. After a year feeling this way, I
decided that I have had enough. I could not endure it anymore. I was
barely eating and would be lucky to get two hours of broken sleep
for the night. For me, other than the painful thoughts, the lack of
sleep really pushed me over the edge because my mind did not have
any downtime.

I did not share my thoughts or feelings with anyone about the
ugly mess of my marriage falling apart and not seeing my children
on a regular basis. No, I just kept it all bottled up inside. I was filled
with bitterness and pain—but mostly pain—so I had no interest in
talking to anyone.

Suicide is a permanent solution to a temporary problem, but at
the time, my mind could not see beyond the dark clouds and pain. I
now know Satan wanted me to kill myself because he knew God had
plans for me to touch many people through the reading of this book
to lead them to Christ our Savior.

My attempt at suicide ended with my having severe stomach
pain and a visit to the emergency room. I tried to fall asleep peace-
fully, but the way I see it now, the Lord was telling me, "It's time
for you to get off the bench and get in the game." So I ended up in

the hospital, having my stomach pumped, feeling embarrassed and shameful.

I remember one of the nurses being pretty stern with me about attempting suicide. She did not know me, yet she showed concern in a tough love kind of way. I'm glad she was there because this was just what I needed at the time because I was wallowing in self-pity. I thought, at the age of twenty-seven, my life was not worth living anymore, but God was going to prove me wrong through this amazing journey he would lead me on, and in the process of finding the Lord, I found myself, and with that came meaning and purpose for living.

"See the light that does exist in the dark. Follow it." The same way God has plans for me, he has plans for you, so when times get hard, and they will, remember, everything is seasonal. Dark clouds will eventually give way to sunshine, and winter will give way to summer. You never know what God has in mind for you, but you need to be here to find out.

Let me share my story with you of how God took me from "broken to blessed," and I hope that it gives you encouragement in your dark, troubled times to stand strong in the Lord our God.

CHAPTER 1

The Calling

Listen to me, o coastlands and give attention you peoples
from afar. The Lord called me from the womb, from
the body of my mother he named my name.

—Isaiah 49:1

When I was three to five years of age, I remember watching a church program on the television where a man on the program was saying, "If you want to accept the Lord as your Savior, repeat after me." I did not even know who I was at this tender age, but I did have a deep desire to know who this one is whom they call God. I placed my small hand on the television screen and repeated after him.

When I look back on this moment, I believe I had that desire to know God because I already knew him in a spiritual sense. I came from him. He is my Creator, and therefore, I was naturally drawn to him.

> For those whom he fore knew he also predestined to be conformed to the image of his son, in order that he might be the firstborn among many brothers. (Romans 8:29)

It would be years before I got to know the Lord, but I don't think it was a coincidence that this program just happened to be on the TV. I think God was reaching out to me at this young age to begin preparation for the journey ahead of me. I was born March 24, 1967, on Good Friday. My mother gave me the name Jerome, which is of Greek origin, meaning "sacred name." I don't think she gave me this name because I was born on Good Friday, nor do I think she knew the meaning of the name.

I remember telling my mother I wanted to go to church when I was a child, and she had no problem taking me, and it just so happened that her father, my grandfather, was a deacon at this church. Some of my fondest childhood memories are from time spent at this church, the Union Baptist Temple in Bridgeton, New Jersey.

I would go to church, but I certainly was not a saint. I remember stealing chocolates and cookies from the local A&P grocery store, starting fights in school, and being known as a bully. While in kindergarten, I showed out so much in class, the school thought it best that I repeat kindergarten. I had to repeat fourth grade as well for the same style of foolish behavior. My first year in fourth grade, I managed to get all Fs on my report card in every subject in every single marking period. I was a hot mess.

One summer, my cousin and I cruised around the neighborhood on our bikes, shooting out car windows and the nearby school windows with some remarkable slingshots his mother bought us, not realizing how deviant our little minds were at the time. Sorry, Aunt Vera, and sorry, Mom.

As the years went by and I hit my early teens, I started to mellow out and mature some, I wanted to finish school, and I was already two years behind, so I began to take church a bit more seriously, and I did not want to give my mother any more problems.

After high school, I did not attend church as often. As a matter of fact, my last two years in high school, I started having more interest in girls than going to church. One day, I was walking down the street near my church, when a car pulled up on the side of me. It was driven by one of the ministers of my church. He rolled his window down and began to question me about why I had not been coming to church. I don't remember the response I gave him, but whatever it was, it just did not cut it for him. He was talking to me in a raised voice, and by the way he expressed himself, it sounded and looked as if he was angry with me when he said, "I'm going to pray that your life is miserable so that you will come back to the Lord."

I don't think his intentions were to make me afraid of him, but he did. I avoided him after that, and I felt a certain way toward him for a very long time.

I want to make it perfectly clear. At this point, I did not know God on a personal level. I barely knew myself on a personal level. Two years after high school, I met the mother of my two children, and a year later, we got married, and with that, I found myself looking for God again. I'm a father now. I need leadership from my God if I'm going to lead a family. So I began to question and wonder how this relationship with God really works.

At twenty-three, I had a moral compass, but I did not always use it. I wanted to know him on an intimate level, but I had no idea how to get there. Now when I look back, I can imagine God watching me and waiting for his planned introduction.

Three years into the marriage, and it had fallen apart for various reasons, but lack of maturity played a major factor. We went through the classic drama associated with divorce (fighting, custody, and child support) and a trip to the county jail for me. When I look back on this moment, I should have walked away, but my stupid young pride got in the way.

I got physical with her, and the cops came for a visit. The next thing I knew, I was eating brown bag lunches at the county jail. I was placed in a not-so-spacious holding cell when I first arrived. Problem was there were two guys already inside this now-even-smaller space. After eight hours in the holding cell, I was taken to a location where I was to remove all of my clothes and have an anal cavity search done. I'm sure this is normal procedure at any jail or prison, but it was not normal for me.

I take full responsibility for my actions that day. My getting angry was one thing; my reaction was yet another. My actions were wrong regardless of what she did or said. There were many lessons for me to learn from this incident, but the one that comes to mind—and I still live by it today—is no matter what a person says or does, if you allow them to get into your head and take you somewhere you should not be, you are now complicit, and depending on your response, you can either go home or you can go to jail.

When you think about it, we should be embarrassed when we allow someone to disturb us so much that we become out of character and lose control. It's a movement of our own thoughts, emotions, and reactions. This takes place in our minds.

Two days later, I had to appear before the judge in my Sunday best outfit: the typical orange jumpsuit, handcuffs, and leg irons. The judge asked me, did I have the $500 bail in order to be released, and I told him I did not have the money. His response was, "Then you will sit in jail until you come up with the money."

I reached out to my mother to inform her of my situation, and my sister offered to loan me the money. I thanked her, and then I told her, "I got myself in this, I will get myself out of it."

When I look back on this moment, I think how crazy I was to turn that money down because I did not have five hundred dollars stashed anywhere, nor did I have any plans on how to get my hands on that kind of money. It was in God's hands now.

After three days in the county, one of the officers called me over to inform me I was being released. When I got outside, I was looking to see who bailed me out, but there was no one to be found, only the night sky with the moon looking down at me. All I could do was worry and pray while I sat in jail, thinking of how this would affect my relationship with my family and my future. It was hard for me to keep my head up and have hope. I was looking at a felony charge. I later found out that my wife dropped the charges with no persuading on my part because I had not spoken to her while I was incarcerated.

Young ladies and young men, with your whole life ahead of you, keep in mind that your future depends on your character. I'm grateful that she had a change of heart and dropped the charges, but I believe the Lord was behind her change of heart, and I boldly say that because God had plans for me to travel the world and to share his Word with people from many different countries and cultures, but I had no clue of this. I was just getting out of jail and about to go through a deep state of depression and an attempt to take my own life.

What made the situation worse after getting out of jail was returning to work because my wife and I worked at the same place but different job duties. What I did not expect upon my return to work was for my personal business to be the current topic of conversation among my colleagues. We are talking at least a thousand employees. It was the walk of shame. All eyes were on me. I remember many people giving me a cold stare, and one female just had to open her mouth to remind me (as if I had forgotten) of my actions that got me sent to jail. People distanced themselves from me like I was a disease they did not want to catch.

One thing this experience taught me was who my real friends were. I already went before the judge, yet society had to have its say on the matter. This just added to the issues I was already dealing with. I was still trying to process this whole ugly situation of going to jail, not seeing my children on a daily basis, the marriage falling apart, then to go back to work and to be picked apart by my coworkers! Each of these circumstances led me further and further down a rabbit hole, which I was beginning to feel there was no way out of.

Never in my life had I ever felt so alone, abandoned, despised, and humiliated. I sat at my mother's apartment, drowning in my tears. I was at rock bottom and ready to tap out on life. What I did not know was that behind the scenes, Jesus was clearing a path that led straight to him. He started with cleaning up the mess I made by getting me out of jail. He "redeemed my mistake." He was setting me on course toward the purpose he birthed me for, that which he planned before I was born but I had no clue at the time. This was showing me that when God has plans for your life, he's going to see to it that you are in position for his purpose, even if he has to bail you out of jail so that you can be readily available for his plans. So even though I screwed up and got myself locked up, God rerouted me back to purpose.

From the time my colleagues walked away from me at my place of work, it began a season of God sweeping people out of my life, but it was for a greater cause—his cause. I was too busy to notice what God was doing in my life, busy dealing with the consequences that remained and the depression that attached itself to them. There are essential ingredients in my personality and character that I'm convinced I would not have today had I not gone through such adversities, which proves to me God can take your ugliest moments and make something blossom from them.

> Behold, I have refined thee, but not with silver,
> I have chosen thee in the furnace of affliction.
> (Isaiah 48:10)

CHAPTER 2

Suicide

I am not at ease or quiet, I have no rest, for trouble has come.

—Job 3:26

Darkness was everywhere, except when I tried to sleep. My mind would light up and repeatedly play the current events that were holding my mind hostage. I felt so lost and alone, as if no one saw me as I walked the streets. Truth is I could not see them because my mind was focused on one thing, so all the people and cars moving past me were nonexistent. The only thing I gave attention to were these painful thoughts that constantly attacked my mind, and I could not make it stop! When I could not get any sleep due to this painful playlist in my mind, I would just lie there and cry.

> I am weary with my groaning, all the night make
> I my bed to swim, I water my couch with tears.
> (Psalm 6:6)

I withdrew from everyone to sit alone, talk to God, and cry. At this point in my life, I still had not found this God I was looking for. I was dealing with the biggest crisis of my life, and I needed him, and I needed him now! I quit my job without informing my employer, but everyone knew why I quit. Then I picked up the habit of drinking alcohol to numb my mind during the day and to help me sleep at night. All hope faded away. I was lost in myself.

> What strength do I have that I should still hope?
> What is my future that I should be patient? (Job 6:11)

The devil knew who I was long before I did. He also knew my playlist, "how I was thinking." I'm sure he wrote the soundtrack! He knew I was weak, frustrated, tired, and ready to give up. I was at the end of myself and could not see myself facing another day of the pain, so I left goodbye notes and gifts to a few friends.

What I thought would be a peaceful transition turned out to be anything but that. I ended up in the emergency room with severe stomach cramps and had to get my stomach pumped. I was released from the hospital the following day, and my family was notified. There was one nurse who spoke to me, and she gave me the tough love that I needed to hear. She lay into me for trying to kill myself at twenty-seven years old, regardless of the circumstances. I thought of her deep, compassionate words and her facial expressions as she stood at the foot of my hospital bed after my release; it gave me hope.

Looking back on the moment, the fact that I did not die, I believe, was divine intervention, and the presence of this compassionate loving nurse, I also think, was divine intervention. I did not see it then, but I see it now. Maybe you will agree as the journey progresses.

One of my failures through this whole mess was not having someone to talk to, to vent to, to release to. I kept it all to myself, which led me to imploding. When God snatched me from death, he had someone right there to talk to me, someone who got my attention, and someone who knew what to say. If you're going through a difficult time right now and you're having trouble with it alone, I pray that you seek help from a friend, family, or if need be, professional help. We are not wired to handle everything alone. Don't do as I did and give up on life because our troubles are seasonal. Your dark clouds will give way to sunshine, and your winters will give way to summer. There is something on the other side of your troubles, and God wants you here to see it. God loves you, and I love you too.

> The thief cometh not, but for to steal, and kill
> and to destroy: I am come that they might have
> life, and that they might have it more abundantly.
> (John 10:10)

AUTHENTIC JEANSWEAR CO.
GNG
JEANS
ESTABLISHED 1993

MPT 7062
NGO
MPT

Jerome Petty
Worlds tallest building

CHAPTER 3

The Move

After some time, I got back on my feet and began to feel better about being in the land of the living. I still was not seeing my children on a regular basis, and that bothered me more than anything. There was a lot of back-and-forth to court, and in the long run, the children were the ones to suffer the most from it. I was trying so hard to help my children adjust to this new living arrangement where when I did see them, it was on the weekends. They spent more time with the sitter than they did with me because I had to work on the weekends, so I would only have about two hours to spend with them when I got home before it was time for bed.

I had no place to stay, so I ended up back home with Mom, but at one point, I was bouncing between my mother's house and my sister's because I felt like I was interrupting their lives with all of my drama. They did not have to tell me. I knew I was, so at times, I would stay at a friend's place or my cousin's and bunk on the couch. Since I felt that I was a bother to folks, I ended up driving around with everything I owned in the back of my SUV. This way, I was prepared no matter whose house I stayed at.

When I finally got an apartment, I was trying to make my kids feel at home in the shabby place with no cable, barely any food, and not much for them to do. All their toys and luxuries were at their mother's place. I could not afford to buy new toys, cable for the TV. I did not even have a phone.

One day, they were at my apartment with me, and they started crying because they wanted to go home. They did not like what little

I had to offer them. Everything they were used to and wanted were at their mother's home, and quite frankly, I could not compete with that. I held it in as long as I could, then I just broke down and cried right in front of my babies. That must have been something for them to see, their father broken to the point of crying aloud in front of them. Only when my baby girl came over to me and placed her hand on my shoulder and said, "Don't cry, Daddy," did I begin to regain my composure.

I remember hearing some years later, "We can remember experiences better because we remember how they feel." I don't think I will ever forget how I felt that day, crying in front of my children with everything weighing heavily on my mind. It's hard to see yourself beyond situations like this. I finally came to the point where I stopped going to pick them up. I could not endure any more of their crying, and it hurt me to feel rejected by my own children. I decided to back off and give them some time, but there were times when they were kept from me. After a few years went by and my children still clung to their mother and things did not appear to be getting any better, I decided to get a fresh start and moved out of New Jersey.

The heart of man plans his way, but the Lord establishes his steps. (Proverbs 16:9)

It was in the move where God got me alone with him, away from all the distractions, drama, and everyone I knew. When I arrived in Savannah, Georgia, I was broken mentally, emotionally, spiritually, and financially. It was at this time I recommitted my life to the Lord, and I was determined more than ever to seek him out and truly get to know him for myself.

Adding to my list of problems that I brought along with me from back home, someone in New Jersey had stolen my identity and was getting felony charges and warrants in my name. In my walk with God, I have learned to love him for who he is, not for what he can do for me, but when I was at this low point, I was looking for a miracle. I wanted God to come quickly to my rescue, but he was in no rush. Based on the way my life was going, it looked as if the Lord had answered the prayer of that minister and allowed misery to have its way with me.

After a year staying with my brother and sister-in-law, I moved into a trailer park in a quiet wooded area. I was doing all I could to not sit in that trailer with no cable, Internet, or anything to do, but I had no money, so I was eventually forced to sit at home on my off days from work. This is where God wanted me to be, but at the time, I could not see it or understand it. If you're around too much noise, distractions, or like in my case in Jersey, too much drama, you will not hear his voice. He was positioning me for solitude, alone time with him. He led me to a silent place where I could hear him. "God is found in solitude."

Once I started hearing from God, I knew he led me to Savannah. He led me to this trailer, and he led me to this deep state of solitude with him. I began to fill myself with his Word and spend much time in prayer, putting God first in my life. For the first time in my life, I was hearing from the Lord through dreams, from the Bible, and through circumstances.

The key to my coming out of my state of depression was experiencing God for myself, not hearing about God but hearing from God himself. This changed everything! God started working on my thought life. When you change the way you think, you automatically change the way you feel and behave. For me, the changing of my thought life has been a lot of work but well worth the effort. I was thirty-three years old at this time, and my thought life and emotional life were a hot mess. Some of my dysfunctions were thirty-three years in the making, so it was not going to be an overnight fix. This was where I got to know God on a more intimate level, in the walking with God while in the process of change for the past twenty-two years.

> Do not be conformed to this world, but be transformed by the renewal of your mind, that by testing you may discern what is the will of God, what is good and acceptable and perfect. (Romans 12:2)

One night, I had a dream. In the dream, I was walking along the beach, and as I tried to walk from one side of the beach to the other, waves of water would rush up on the beach in front of me to prevent me from moving forward. Then over the ocean, I saw a waterspout, and as it got closer, it turned into a rod or staff. What I gathered from the dream upon awakening was that your journey will be rough, but I will be with you.

I had to work two jobs for a while to make ends meet. I did not have a college education, trade, or a military background, so it was hard to find a decent-paying job being the new guy in town. Then I landed a job as a correctional officer at a youth detention facility. I was excited about working with the youth, and the pay was better than most of the jobs offered to me. It was a steady job, and I thought it was honorable work giving guidance and direction to our troubled youth.

When I say youth detention facility, I think what comes to mind for most people is sweet little boys who have stepped off the path and need a gentle nudge in the right direction. After all, this is what I thought I was signing up for. Not even close! We had kids coming in with gunshot wounds! The wounds were healed over, "but they were gunshot wounds!"

The majority of them were in gangs, so there were violent fights quite often. As a matter of fact, in all my youthful fights, I never tried to hurt anyone as badly as these kids went after each other. It was vicious and dangerous. Not only dangerous for the kids, it was dangerous for the officers also.

For you to get a better understanding of what I mean by *dangerous*, let me break it down. I stood five feet seven inches tall at 180 pounds. One of the boys stood six feet four inches and weighed in at 240 pounds! I looked like an ant standing next to him. I would be on a unit with twenty to twenty-five teenage boys by myself, and from time to time, it got violent, and with my stepping in to break up fights, I would get injured at times.

It did not take long for me to realize that the dream I had was revelation for this youth facility. I did train in the gym, so I had a muscular frame, and I was pretty strong, so in the beginning, I used that to my advantage until I came across a kid who was not impressed. As a matter of fact, he got very rude and disrespectful with his choice of words toward me one evening. I had experienced much disrespect from these young men, but in the end, a level of respect was established, but there was something different about this kid, but I know now it was a learning opportunity for me, for God was about to show me it was not by my might or power but by his Spirit that I would succeed. I prayed about the situation, asking for guidance, and the Lord led me to a scripture in Zechariah.

> Not by might, nor by power, but by my Spirit
> saith the Lord of host. (Zechariah 4:6)

I was relying on my might and power to control these young men, but the Lord was telling me I would succeed by his Spirit.

A few days had passed before I had to work on the unit where this young man was housed. I went to him and asked him if he believed in the Lord God, and he immediately dropped his head and, to my surprise, told the other boys not to give me any more trouble. From then on, I talked to them about our Lord and Savior and how to invite him into their lives.

In time, I noticed a difference in some of the boys. They began showing me their softer side, letting their guards down. Many of them craved a father figure, and one kid I remember in particular, his mother was going through a bad time, and he thought that I could be the man to make her life better. He got teased by the other kids for trying to hook me up with his mom, but I was and still am truly flattered.

They started to open up to me, telling me some of the bad things that they had done and wondered if God would forgive them, and I assured them that he would. Although it was still challenging, it had started to become a rewarding experience. There were times I would get down on my knees alongside some of the boys and pray with them before bed, then at other times, when they were tucked in bed, I would sing for them.

One of their favorite songs was "A Change Is Gonna Come" by Sam Cooke. It was also one of my favorites, so I felt honored when they asked me to sing this song for them. When I sang that song, the boys would be so quiet, you could hear a pin drop in between the verses. As it turned out, there still was a sweet little boy inside these young men, but to get to it, you had to get them to lower their defenses, and the Lord knew just how to accomplish that: by his Spirit.

Working at the detention facility stayed a continual challenge due to the simple fact that new inmates were coming in weekly, if not daily, so the process repeated itself. I worked at the detention facility for three years, but at the two-year mark, I began looking for work elsewhere because of the physical and mental demands of the detention facility. The only problem with my plan was God still had work for me at the detention facility with the boys.

At the time, I was still learning how to walk with God, so I was new at working under God's timing, which means God sent me to the detention facility on assignment, and that assignment was not completed until he said so, not because I got tired of it or it stressed me out. This was kingdom work, so when I broke down in tears before the Lord in prayer, hoping he would feel sorry for me and get me out of there, I got silence from the Lord.

> Many are the plans in a person's heart, but it is
> the Lords purpose that prevails. (Proverbs 19:21)

The Lord did send seasons of refreshment when I did not have to work with the boys directly on a day-to-day basis, which took some of the load off, but by the time my third year came around, I was back working with the boys daily. My season of refreshment had come and gone. What I did not know was that the Lord was making plans for my departure. You cannot convince me that this was not the hand of the Almighty God!

One day while on duty at the detention facility, there was a new employee speaking with some of my colleagues about his previous job. His previous job was a federal contractor, providing armed security on a US Army base in Kosovo, Europe. When I saw him alone, I inquired about his previous position. He filled me in on the details and requirements, which included shooting range qualifications, self-defense course, PT test, written exam, psyche eval. But what stood out among the requirements was three years' experience in law enforcement, military, or corrections. I had just completed my third year!

What also came to mind was maybe God had me stay at this job for three years so I could be qualified for this new position. Could this be why God was silent when I prayed to him about moving on from the detention facility, because he already had something in mind for me? I made several attempts to get employment elsewhere, but no one would hire me. Was this the reason God blocked me from leaving? I was full of excitement, but I had to calm myself. After all, I was not sure if God was behind this.

I prayed on the move, then, within a few days, called the number that was provided by the new employee. I spoke with a recruiter for the company, and after we exchanged information, he asked me if I had a valid passport. I took the steps to purchase a passport, and within three weeks, I was on an airplane, flying international for the first time in my life.

With the feeling of confidence, with the timing of the messenger (the new employee), with the three years needed in corrections and how God saw to it that no one would hire me when I tried to leave, to the recruiter sending my itinerary, it all lined up like confirmation. God is awesome!

I was confident, but that does not mean I was not afraid. Sometimes, we can let fear talk us out of an opportunity to experience God. Yes, I was afraid because I still had to pass all my training requirements, get to know my new colleagues, and be in a new country not knowing anyone! To have more, you have to become more, so I chose to face my fears.

I did believe God was behind this opportunity, but I felt I was being taken out of my comfort zone. I was giving God control, and it can feel scary giving up control of your life and not knowing where God is leading you until you learn to rest in him, knowing he only plans what's best for you. It's only when we face life's challenges that we spiritually grow.

The flight gave me plenty of time to think of the past three years at the detention facility and all the challenges that came with it and how God saw me through every one of them. I realized I had to take this same frame of mind with me to my future on the other side of the Atlantic Ocean.

CHAPTER 4

The Catapult

After arriving and meeting the other recruits, I was convinced that there must have been a mistake for my being there. This job was armed security on a US Army base, and it seemed all my fellow recruits were qualified with law enforcement and military backgrounds, and here I was with youth corrections and casino security under my belt. I felt totally unqualified. I kid you not. For the first three months I was there, I was waiting for someone from management to inform me they made a mistake hiring me.

This was the beginning of many moments when God would thrust me into something that I felt totally unqualified for, and he knew I would feel unqualified, but this was the bread and butter I needed to establish trust and faith in my Lord. God can see things in you that you can't see yourself, and God will never demand from you that he did not put in you.

When I was trying to leave the detention facility and find another job on my own, I was attempting to get a job at one of the local stores, but God was showing me I was not thinking big enough. The plans he had for me were things I could not imagine for myself, not with my limited skills. I think God showed up and started blessing me beyond my dreams for various reasons, but these reasons stood out to me: to fulfill his purpose, to cast out any doubt in my mind of his existence, to show me he is God Almighty and in control of all my circumstances, and to show me I'm bigger than I think of myself because he has my back.

After completing all the required training, I was added to the work schedule. Prior to working this job, I worked eleven years in Atlantic City, New Jersey, as a security officer and three years at the detention facility. This was a major jump as for job responsibilities, and it was a major jump financially. I was living paycheck to paycheck the whole time I worked at the detention facility, and it was not due to bad budgeting practices. I was still in a financial hole that I came to Savannah with. My biweekly pay was double that which I made at the detention facility, and with the new company covering my food cost and lodging, I was able to get caught up pretty quickly on all of my outstanding debt.

With God, the shift started with my head. Now he was helping me with circumstances. I am still blown away to this very day as to how he took me from being broken spiritually, mentally, financially, and emotionally. After several months at the new job, I was asked if I would like to work at the main office as an assistant for the shift supervisor. I once read God will purposely put you in situations where you're over your head, where no one can help you, where you don't have the experience.

I was honored that they offered me the position, but again, the unqualified bells began to ring loudly because I had no computer skills at that time. I did not know how to respond because I was embarrassed to tell them that I lacked computer skills. Out of all my colleagues, I'm sure majority of them had computer skills and were more qualified, but truth be told, it was God choosing me for the position, not the shift supervisor, and I knew it was him. I had just started to feel comfortable with the new position, then God showed up and started making me uncomfortable, but there was purpose behind it because everything I did not want to do is what got me where I am today, talking to you!

I did not want the position because of my fear of failure, but I accepted it because it was clear to me God had chosen me for this position. When you start your journey with God, expect to be challenged. It's God's way of preparing and positioning you. When the Lord positioned me at the detention facility, he provided me with everything I needed. Now I was put in a position where I had to practice my faith that he would provide yet again.

> Commit to the Lord whatever you do and all
> your plans will succeed. (Proverbs 16:3)

Even though I felt God was behind this, I prayed about it anyway for confirmation. I have to commend the shift supervisor for being very patient with me and supportive and never seemed bothered even when I asked the same questions over and over. The support I received from shift supervisors Brent Farmer and Antonio Farmer, along with help from two of my colleagues Carl Williams and Edward Jones, was just what I needed to get me up to speed. Now I'm used to being pushed out of my comfort zone by God, and it's taking me to new levels of growth that my prayers have changed from, "Make it easy and painless for me, Lord," to "Do whatever you see fit with your servant, Lord God."

> As for me, behold, I am in your hands: do with
> me as seems good and proper to you. (Jeremiah
> 26:14)

After a year working in our main office, the shift supervisor talked to me about applying for a security clearance. A security clearance is a status granted to individuals, allowing them access to classified information following an intensive background check. Usually, you can see an increase in pay with a security clearance also. I was sure I would be denied the clearance because of the issue with someone in my home state of New Jersey stealing my identity and dragging my name through the mud.

At one point while I was still living in Jersey, a detective called me at my job to inform me he had two warrants in my name that totaled $4,000; and on a separate charge sometime later, there were forgery and drug charges, and I can't begin to count all the traffic violations. These were the charges I knew of. God only knows how many there were.

After some persuading by the shift supervisor, I applied for the clearance. God had brought me this far against all odds. As I said earlier, it's an intensive background check, so it can take several months to get a security clearance, but when it was all said and done, I was granted my security clearance. God is awesome! I found out later that the police were on to this individual running around using my name.

> What then shall we say to these things? If God is
> for us who can be against us? (Romans 8:31)

After my suicide attempt, when I was trying to get back on my feet, I remember walking my mother to work one day and telling her that I wanted a job that was special and not open to just anyone. At the time, I was still unemployed, drinking too much, and battling depression, so when we reached her place of work and I turned to head back home, the dark clouds of despair swooped down on me, as if to say, "You're not going anywhere. I own you, so get those foolish thoughts out of your mind," and I let despair have its way with me that day.

> Take delight in the Lord, and he will give you the
> desires of your heart. (Psalm 37:4)

I already felt like I was blessed beyond my dreams with this job in Europe, but when I obtained the security clearance, it took me up another level. After five years and six months working armed security on the US military base in Europe, I decided to move on to another company. At the new job, I was also providing security for US installations overseas as well. For my first assignment, I was sent to Jeddah, Saudi Arabia. At the new job, I was making five times my biweekly pay at the detention facility.

Everything I share with you of how God has blessed me beyond measure is just that. God did this. I did not do any of this in my own power or might. I was completely broken in every area of my life until God showed up, so for the record, I'm not boasting. If anything, I'm boasting about the power of God. I just want you to see how God took someone broken down like myself and completely changed my life.

From time to time, I have thought to myself why the Lord has been so kind and loving to me. It's not like I deserve it. I have sinned. I have done my share of wrong, but that's not to say that the Lord did not correct or discipline me.

> For it is by grace you have been saved through faith. And this is not your own doing, it is the gift of God, not a result of works, so that no one may boast. (Ephesians 2:8–10)

While I was working in Saudi Arabia, I discovered the Red Sea was walking distance from my hotel, the same Red Sea that God parted for the Israelites to walk through on dry land, the same Red Sea where the Egyptian Army of six hundred chariots chased after them when they fled Egypt, the same Red Sea that crashed down on the Egyptians and drowned them. I could not believe God had brought me to a place where he had shown one of his most powerful miracles to mankind.

I was truly touched and humbled by the experience. It felt like God led me here. That's what made it more meaningful. So I could not pass up the opportunity to put my feet in the same waters as Moses and the Israelites. For me, this was a sacred moment, a baptism even. Several years ago, I was trying to kill myself. I could not see what was waiting on the other side of those dark clouds, but God could! On the other side of disappointment, we can often see that our disappointment led us to our destiny. All good times and bad times have an expiration date. There is something finished that you were born to start. There is something God wanted done that requires your existence. That's why I'm still standing.

After I completed my one-year stay in Saudi Arabia, I decided to stay in America for a while. I applied for a civilian job on a US Army base in Georgia. The odds were against me being that the other applicants were retired military, but God showed up and showed out again! While I was home at this time back in America, a good friend of mine passed away, so I took the twelve-hour drive back to New Jersey for his funeral.

I never have been comfortable around crowds or walking into a crowded room. I get nervous and don't know what to do with myself, so the thought of speaking to a crowded room, I might black out! I have been in situations where I was asked a question in a room of four or more people, and my brain would shut down. Verbal fluency goes straight to zero. It's embarrassing, to say the least, but I usually manage to find some words to respond back that probably had nothing to do with the question. This is how bad I was at the time heading to this funeral. I have since learned to be more relaxed around people, but I still don't do crowds so well.

So while I was driving to Jersey, I said to myself, if they open the floor for anyone to say a few words, I would go up and say something. I felt the need to say something because Mike Burrus was, quite frankly, the best man I have ever known. The way he carried himself, his character was exceptional. Without talking to him, you could tell he was a God-fearing man.

As I got to know him better, I thought to myself, *What he has in his character, I want some of that!* He made a major impact on who I am today, and that was because God allowed us to cross paths in this brief moment of life. I got to know him on a personal level, and we were good friends for years, so even though I might freeze up in front of a crowded room, I felt compelled to say something. This is how much he meant to me. I would take that risk.

And of course, since the Lord heard me say, "If they open the floor for guests to speak, I would say a few words," he made sure that happened. I stood up and walked over to the line where people were waiting to go up front to speak in this crowded room, and let me tell you, I was in panic mode. I could not hear anything from the person up front speaking because I was in fight-or-flight mode. My mind was totally focused on surviving the moment in front of all those people. All those eyes looking directly at me. Then I turned to monkey mind. My mind was all over the place, jumping form one thought to the next. I had nothing prepared. I was just going to wing it when I knew my verbal fluency has a way of going to zero around crowds.

As I took the floor before the crowd, I began speaking about Mike's passing and that I had to make the trip up from Georgia for his funeral, and just like that, the Holy Spirit kicked in and took over the speech (this had never happened to me before). I did not have to think of what to say. The words came naturally, and I was calm and relaxed. I barely remember anything I said, as this was some years ago, but my verbal fluency was flowing off the charts. At times, I was using words that I don't normally use in my vocabulary. I remember speaking on Mike's exceptional character and the crowd nodding their heads in agreement. I also remember getting a slight chuckle from the crowd, which I believe came from my facial expressions or my explosive way of presenting my words and gestures.

Upon closing my speech, they gave me a round of applause, something I did not see for any other speaker, not to downplay or disrespect anyone else who spoke that day or to make myself sound special. I don't take credit for the speech. That was the Holy Spirit, and I thank him for showing up. It was God showing me he is the Creator of tongues, and it showed me how he can show up where I'm weak.

When I got back to my seat and reality set in as to what had just happened, the adrenaline rush kicked back in, and I probably was looking crazy for several minutes. After nine months working on the US Army base in Georgia, I decided I wanted to do more international work and travel. My work took me to the countries of Kosovo for five years and six months, Saudi Arabia for one year and a second trip to Saudi Arabia for eleven months, Laos for one year, Afghanistan for three years, Croatia for three months, and to Mozambique, Africa, for three and a half years.

While I was in Africa, I had the opportunity to visit Cape Town, which is located at the southern tip of the continent of Africa, where the Atlantic Ocean meets the Indian Ocean. The beaches and mountains made some of the most beautiful landscapes I have ever seen. Just off the coast of Cape Town, just under four miles, lies Robben Island, where Nelson Mandela was held as a prisoner for eighteen years of his twenty-seven-year imprisonment. I had the opportunity to visit Robben Island and stood in front of the very cell that was Mandela's home for eighteen years. I walked the same corridors as Mandela and stood on the same courtyard they used for physical exercise. This was yet another moving and humbling experience that I'm grateful God shared with me.

These are moments and experiences that are beyond anything I ever imagined for myself. I was a poor kid growing up in Bridgeton, New Jersey, the last born of five children, no college degree, no trade skills, no military background, and God said, "I choose you." It does not matter where you are from or what you lack. If God decides to use you, he will make you qualified wherever he sends you.

Going to Africa alone was a huge moment for me. I felt as if I was being welcomed home in Mozambique. "Welcome back home to the motherland of your ancestors." I did not want to leave, and it was the hardest country for me to leave behind. I will cherish this experience for the rest of my life.

> Now unto him that is able to do exceeding abun-
> dantly above all that we ask or think, according
> to the power that worketh in us. (Ephesians 3:20)

If I had been successful in killing myself, I would have never known that God had plans to use me and bless me beyond my wildest dreams. When I turned my life over to Christ, I just wanted him to heal my troubled mind and mend my broken heart, but as you can see, God had a lot more in mind than just a healing. I believe the Lord had this journey prepared for me before I was born.

> Your eyes saw my unformed substance, in your
> book were written, every one of them, the days
> that were formed for me, when as yet there was
> none of them. (Psalm 139:16)

Now that the veil has been removed, I can see the people God put in my life to shape me, the good and the bad. I now can clearly see the minister—who prayed for me to be miserable so that I would return to the Lord—really cared about me. He scared me with his approach, but I'm grateful for his prayer. I'm also able to see God in the circumstances from my past where he provided provisions, protection, correction, discipline, and blessings. I can also see where he removed people out of my life so I could fulfill my purpose or, in some cases, to protect me from them.

There have been many times in my fifty-five years on this earth I have fallen and gone through setbacks, hardships, beatdowns, and God has always been there to see me through. Not once has he failed me, even when I got arrogant and prideful because the Lord was blessing me beyond measure and started acting as if I had done things in my own power.

"I got cocky, like I made this happen!" Pride comes before the fall. He let me fall flat on my face with circumstances until I was humbled. Then like a caring father helping his child up off the ground after he crashed his bicycle, God helped me to my feet, cleared the dust off my pants, and set me on my way back to purpose, his purpose. God is committed to his investment. Whatever he allows to happen in my life, I trust that I need it somehow. Whether I like it or not is irrelevant. If he allowed it, I trust him.

God has a journey in mind for you also. Your journey will be unique to you as mine is unique to me. After walking through multiple beatdowns, circumstances, heartbreaks, and crushing moments from life, God has healed me and delivered me from it all. Now when I face difficult times, God knows all about it. He allowed it. My job is to trust him, and because I do trust him, I live in peace.

> He who heeds the word wisely will find good, and whoever trust in the Lord happy is he. (Proverbs 16:20)

Whenever God is allowing trouble, this is how I view it: "Whatever needs to be done, no matter how painful, no matter how troubling, Lord, do it to make me what you want me to be so that when it's all said and done, I will hear, 'Well done, thy good and faithful servant!'" The very thing that I tried to kill myself over, the hardships of life, is the same thing that has turned me into the warrior I am today.

Claim your brokenness as you do your blessings. Embrace the suffering and adapt. I'm human, so at times, problems catch me off guard, and I find myself worrying until I regain my focus on the Lord, the Rock. I have learned to wear my pain and suffering as a badge of honor in my attempt to model my life after Jesus Christ, who went through the ultimate form of suffering for us. How can I complain about what God allows me to go through after what he endured?

It is not how things are but how we see them. Everything is a test. I'm constantly learning and growing with every challenge that God allows to come my way. When I know that I'm living obediently, and all of a sudden, life gets turned upside down, what gives me confidence in those moments is knowing that this particular moment had to be allowed by God, and if he allowed it, he will see me through it. I see my problems as being divinely outmatched because I have the King of kings in my corner. The crushings that God allowed in my life led to the opposite effect.

> And we know that in all things God works for
> the good of those who love him, who have been
> called according to his purpose. (Romans 8:28)

Your difficult times are just as much yours as your blessings. Learn to embrace them both. They both serve a purpose.

> Should we accept from God only good and not
> adversity. (Job 2:10)

Have someone you can open up to and share your feelings. Don't do as I did, holding it all inside, leading me to replay over and over again the soundtrack that Satan wrote just for me. I hope by reading my story, you will realize there is something most precious waiting for you on the other side of your dark moments. I'm confident God feels your pain just like he felt mine. If I had succeeded in killing myself, I would not have been here to reach out to you today. It's no coincidence you're reading this book.

Satan wanted me to kill myself, just like he's convincing millions worldwide to commit suicide. Satan has destroyed his life, and the old saying is "misery loves company." He wants to take as many people as possible with him to his defeat. He wants to destroy your natural life and your eternal life because he knows God loves you and has plans for your life. My circumstances lost their power when I realized God was using them for my benefit. My part is to serve and obey him, and God will have my circumstances serve me. The Holy Spirit has awakened me to who I am in Christ Jesus, so no matter what situation I find myself in, I know that everything I need is inside of me. When you learn who you are in Christ Jesus, you will be able to use adversity for your benefit.

It was twenty-eight years ago when I tried to take my own life. If I had been successful, there would have been so much I would have missed out on. God has blessed me well beyond all I could ever imagine for myself. To make a list of things that I'm grateful for that he has shared with me after rejecting my attempt at suicide and giving me my life back more abundantly (that's a loving Father, by the way), the list would go on and on, but to highlight a few of them, I would have to start out with how I would have missed out on this loving relationship with God Almighty and how he healed my heart and my mind and set me on the path of purpose. He redeemed me and blessed me beyond measure, sharing dreams and soft whispers to my mind. How he made it possible for me to put my feet in the Red Sea and the visiting of the prison that held Nelson Mandela, along with my travels to Africa and all other international travels.

I would have also missed out on becoming the warrior I am today, a servant of the Most High, the King of kings and Lord of lords, Christ Jesus. I would have missed out on my relationship with my daughter being restored. She has a child of her own now, which makes me a grandfather. I also have three grandchildren from my son. I would have missed out on the time spent at the youth detention facility. Although it was challenging, it was a rewarding experience.

Last but not least, I would have missed the joy of sharing my blessings with my mother. I'm so grateful to God that he has put me in a position where I can bless her abundantly after what she had to endure raising five children on her own. It's a blessing to be able to give back to the woman who played a major role in helping me become the person I am today.

The fact that God turned my journey into a book is beyond my wildest dreams, and I would have missed out on this opportunity to tell you about this merciful, loving, kind God who's waiting to hear from you. My friends, if God took a misfit like me—a man who was completely broken in every area of his life, a man who committed much sin in the eyes of the Lord, yet when I humbled myself before his throne, he reached down from the heavens and helped me to my feet, and when everyone else had forsaken me, he held me with a deep embrace—if God did this for me, he will surely provide you with the peace that you seek and much more. Humble yourself before the Lord and watch him move in your life.

> And the peace of God, which surpasses all understanding will guard your hearts and minds through Christ Jesus. (Philippians 4:7)

This level of peace can only be gotten one way: through Christ Jesus. This is where I live today, with my heart and mind in peace. God turned my depression into peace. This is not to say trouble does not pay me a visit from time to time, but when it does show up, it's divinely outmatched because God's in control. If you're going through a difficult time right now, I want you to know, where you are right now is not a permanent situation. God has a purpose for your life. I encourage you to turn your heart and mind over to the Lord and let him turn your brokenness into blessings.

> For God so loved the world, that he gave his only begotten Son, that whosoever believeth in him should not perish, but have everlasting life. (John 3:16)

Nelson Mandela's window, third from the left, over looking a courtyard.

Nelson Mandela's prison cell.

The court yard outside of his window

Now inactive maximum security prison where Mandela was a prisoner.

This view is from Robben Island, and in the distance you can see Cape town, South Africa. To be able to see freedom but not able to experience it must have been extra torment for the prisoners.

MAXIMUM
SECURITY
PRISON

TABLE MOUNTAIN, CAPE TOWN, SOUTH AFRICA.
ableMountain
33 54'30.0" S 18 25'20.1" E

Jerome Petty was born and raised in Bridgeton, New Jersey. At age thirty, he moved to Savannah, Georgia, and soon afterward began a career in security as a force protection specialist (federal contractor) for the Department of Defense and then moved on to construction security as a federal contractor for the US State Department Overseas Building Operations, a career that has spanned nineteen years between the two departments. He currently resides in Forest Park, Georgia.

To contact Mr. Petty he can be reached at jerome6012@yahoo.com and Facebook.

www.ingramcontent.com/pod-product-compliance
Lightning Source LLC
Chambersburg PA
CBHW061132160726
48006CB00036B/1792